No Small Dreams

Florida Institute of Technology, 1958–2008

by Jay Wilson

Copyright © 2008, Florida Institute of Technology
All rights reserved.

Florida Institute of Technology
150 W. University Blvd.
Melbourne, FL 32901

Published in conjunction with

Reedy Press
PO Box 5131
St. Louis, MO 63139

No part of this publication may be reproduced or transmitted in any form or by any means, electronic or mechanical, including photocopy, recording, or any information storage and retrieval system, without permission in writing from the publisher.

Permissions may be sought directly from Reedy Press at the above mailing address or via our website at http://www.reedypress.com.

Library of Congress Cataloging-in-Publication Data: 2008926182

ISBN: 978-1-933370-41-5

For all information on all Reedy Press publications
visit our website at http://www.reedypress.com.

Printed in China
07   08   09   10   11   5   4   3   2   1

To my daughter Miranda and all future generations of Panthers.

For the students, faculty, and staff who lived, learned, and worked together these past 50 years to make Florida Tech the remarkable place it is today.

Contents

vii | Foreword, by Melanie Keuper

viii | Acknowledgments

3 | Sputnick, Pelicans, and the Power of Dreams
Florida Institute of Technology, 1958–1968

25 | Second Stage: A Decade of Growth, Expansion, and Gardening
Florida Institute of Technology, 1968–1978

43 | Traditions and Transition
Florida Institute of Technology, 1978–1988

63 | Reaching for the Stars
Florida Institute of Technology, 1988–1998

75 | The Edge of Discovery
Florida Institute of Technology, 1998–2007

95 | Epilogue: Passing the Torch
Florida Institute of Technology, 2008
by Anthony James Catanese

103 | Appendix A
The Florida Institute of Technology Board of Trustees, March 2008

104 | Appendix B
Five Decades of Florida Institute of Technology Trustees

Foreword

It seems hard to believe that it has been fifty years since my father made good on a 37-cent donation and created Brevard Engineering College out of thin air. I realize now how proud I was, and still am, to be Jerry Keuper's daughter. He was such an extraordinary man. His vision probably scared the heck out of my dear mother. You have to admit, to take 37 cents and start a university is quite out of the ordinary.

Dad dug up my mother's New England roots, where her entire family lived, and moved her to the Mosquito Coast of Florida where there was nothing but sand. Once we found a little home in the sandbox, dad was not home as much as most fathers. He was working for RCA and founding Florida Tech.

I have a number of fond memories about growing up in and around all things Florida Tech. When dad was creating the botanical garden on campus, we would load up the station wagon with new specimens of palm trees that the family had collected and re-plant them in their new campus home. When the weather got cold, we would race back from Melbourne Beach and set out smudge pots. There were always a great number of palms not hardy enough to take our subfreezing temperatures.

There were many occasions when renowned scientists and engineers would visit the university. I distinctly remember Dr. Wernher von Braun and Dr. Edward Teller coming to town. Believe it or not, Dr. von Braun ate tacos at Tippee's Taco House with us.

I suppose the efforts put forth by my parents to found a university were very trying. As a child I didn't recognize the sacrifices that both my parents made. My mother was my father's rock. Without the support of my mom, Natalie, dad could not have achieved the goals that he had set forth.

My brother, Philip, and I helped a bit, too. We listened to speech after speech at the dinner table, and we assured my dad that "it sounds great!" (so we could get back to playing hide and seek in the backyard). This declaration was always followed by mom reporting that it needed a little work.

In short, I feel blessed to have grown up in the BEC, Florida Tech family and to have been able to watch it blossom into full bloom. This book celebrates the first fifty years of dad's vision. I can't wait to see what happens next.

Melanie Keuper
September 1, 2007

Melanie Keuper draws the winning ticket for a 1963 Monza, Brevard Engineering College's first fundraiser. Her brother, Philip, is helping Melanie while father Jerry and Melbourne Businessman Jim Rathmann await the results.

Acknowledgments

Trying to compress fifty years of history into 120 pages would be a Herculean task for any writer but especially for one not trained as a historian. Therefore, I'd like to thank two of Florida Tech's preeminent historians, Gordon Patterson and Robert Taylor, for their invaluable guidance and insight during the formative stages of this work.

Special thanks also to Judi Tintera and Rob Gribbroek in university publications and Ken Droscher, executive director of the alumni association, for their tireless efforts in the archival photo recovery process. As for the photos themselves, countless photographers contributed to the images contained in this book, but special mention should go to Sterling Photo, David Potter, and Barry Eager in producing several of the memorable images contained herein.

I am grateful for the insights of Andy Revay, Harry Weber, Richard Enstice, and Bill Jurgens. Each of these gentlemen was an eyewitness to many events detailed in these pages, and their combined support for this project was a boon for me.

Many thanks also to Celine Lang, dean of libraries, and her entire staff in opening the university's archives to this project. I am indebted to the people who comprise Florida Tech's university communications, my home away from home these past eight years. Karen Rhine, Verna Layman, Melinda Millsap, and Rebecca Vick have all been wonderfully supportive of this effort.

Finally, I'd like to send heartfelt thanks to Thomas G. Fox, the senior vice president for advancement, and Florida Tech President Anthony J. Catanese. Tom provided continued support during the writing of this book, while President Catanese's transformational leadership continues to inspire all who work for him.

Jay Wilson
March 2008

No Small Dreams

Florida Institute of Technology, 1958–2008

Sputnik, Pelicans, and the Power of Dreams
Florida Institute of Technology, 1958–1968

Thirty-seven cents.

This first donation, change from a pay phone call given to young missileman Jerome P. Keuper at the Pelican Bar in Indian Harbour Beach, was the unlikely beginning to the remarkable story that is Florida Institute of Technology. Keuper founded the college, modeled after the Bridgeport (Conn.) Engineering Institute, in an attempt to enhance the qualifications of the scientists and engineers leading America's race for space.

On October 4, 1957, the Soviet Union launched the Sputnik satellite into orbit and the alarm bells rang in America's scientific community. Three months later, America launched Explorer I, just as Keuper, his wife Natalie, and infant daughter Melanie crossed the Florida state line. Keuper had been hired at Cape Canaveral as that site's chief scientist in RCA's Systems Analysis Group.

Earlier in his career, Keuper had taught night courses at the Bridgeport Engineering Institute and was immediately concerned at the lack of higher education resources in East Central Florida. He turned to the founder of BEI, Arthur Keating, and asked if it would be possible to start a branch at the Cape. Keating declined the offer and instructed Keuper to "start your own college."

And that's what Keuper did.

The initial meetings of the first officers of what would become Florida Institute of Technology were held at the Pelican Bar. Joining Keuper in those early meetings were George Peters, Donya Dixon, Robert Kelly, and Harold Dibble. Duties were assigned. Keuper was named president, Dibble the dean, Peters the head of the Mathematics Department, Kelly the chief financial officer, and Dixon the organizational secretary.

In this photo from 1967, Dr. Jerry Keuper leans on the podium as he leads the campus in a dedication of an electrical engineering laboratory in honor of Dr. James Smith.

On September 22, 1958, the first classes were held at Eau Gallie Junior High School. One hundred and fifty-four students enrolled, including six women. The newly dubbed Brevard Engineering College soon received national attention from *Time* and *Newsweek* magazines, both of whom applauded the college's efforts. The next year, the college announced its first formal degree programs, a master of science in space technology and a master of science in applied mathematics.

In 1961, BEC moved into its current Melbourne campus. Construction soon began on administration and classroom buildings. While a permanent home had been found, the college itself was still very much unsettled.

While the college's first degree in 1961 was given to Reagan Dubose, it wasn't until June of 1962 that BEC held its first commencement. It honored a graduating class of thirty-eight. Included among the graduates were the first two honorary doctorates given to Florida Secretary of State Tom Adams and Astronaut Virgil "Gus" Grissom. Grissom was the first NASA astronaut to receive an honorary degree.

That same year, the Melbourne Chamber of Commerce presented Keuper with what appeared to be a financial panacea—a merger with the Disciples of Christ Church. The merger would have transformed BEC into Florida Christian University, similar to the church's Texas Christian University (TCU). While negotiations lasted for nearly a year, the merger ultimately failed for two reasons. First, the church did not bring the financial backing Keuper had been promised by the chamber. Second, the church planned to replace the university's leadership, including Keuper!

Those concerned by the failed merger need not have worried. By 1964, the enrollment at the college had more than tripled, Keuper had committed to building a residential college with the dedication of the first dormitory, Brownlie Hall, and construction was underway on an 11,000 square-foot two-story library. That same year, the college was accredited by the Southern Association of Colleges and Schools.

BEC had truly arrived. It would soon vanish.

By 1966, BEC was no more; the name had permanently changed to Florida Institute of Technology. The new university began to branch out its academic offerings, expanding past the rocket science and engineering curriculums envisioned at the Pelican Bar.

The first change was the creation of a department of oceanography. A year later came a school of aeronautics. Also in 1967, the university celebrated the arts with the dedication of the W. Lansing Gleason Auditorium.

If the curriculum changes began with a trickle, by 1968 they came with a tidal wave. Included in the changes were new centers for pollution research, medical research, and ocean technology. Ground was broken on the university's first athletics complex, the Percy Hedgecock Gymnasium.

What began as a dream in the Pelican Bar came a long way in ten short years. A new university was beginning to form.

And it all began with 37 cents.

SPUTNICK, PELICANS, AND THE POWER OF DREAMS | 5

Left: The Space Coast looked very different in 1958 than it does today. Far from being a desirable place to live, Brevard County was known mostly for alligators and mosquitoes. Local companies, including Radiation, Inc., and RCA embraced the new college as another way to attract talented scientists and engineers to the area.

Right: With the liftoff of Apollo 11, man was on his way to the moon. The decade that preceded this historic achievement was a remarkable one for both the leadership of American ingenuity and the creation of a brand new technological university. During this decade, Jerry Keuper's dreams, and America's, would come true.

Following Page: BEC's first board of trustees meeting occurred on February 25, 1959. At the meeting were, from left, Harold Dibble, Garrett Quick, Clifford Mattox, Jerry Keuper, Norman Lund, and George Shaw.

Year One: This 1959 photograph shows, from left, Reagan Dubose, undergraduate student and RCA technician; President Jerry Keuper; Dean Harold Dibble; Ray Work, graduate student; and Donya Dixon, graduate student and RCA quality analysis scientist. Dixon also served as the college's organizational secretary, while Dubose would earn the fledgling college's first degree. As a faculty member and administrator, Work played an important role in the college's development. As its first dean, Dibble played the lead role in the formation of the college's academic structure.

An otherwise inconspicuous advertisement heralds the first academic term of Brevard Engineering College, left. The company Keuper worked for, RCA, agreed to pay tuition for 75 employees that first semester, ensuring the college a successful start. Three years later, BEC would be teaching classes in its new permanent home on Country Club Drive. Missileman and faculty member Sebastian D'Alli, above, uses the first stage of a Vanguard rocket engine to teach a rocket propulsion class in a new quadrangle classroom. The classroom and the rocket engine are still a part of the Florida Tech campus.

The Florida Tech campus is still home to one of the original University of Melbourne buildings. The bas-relief on the building represents the ideals of that university's founders in the mid-1950s. Today, the building is the home of Human Resources. Named for Florida Tech pioneer, Ray Work, the Work Building is the most aptly named of any campus structure.

This advertisement is the first showcasing BEC's new permanent home.

Preceding page: Before moving to its permanent campus, BEC traveled around the county. The 1960 class shown here was held at Radiation, Inc.

A new administration building was among the first orders of business for Brevard Engineering College once it arrived at its permanent campus.

Keuper's first office in the new administration building.

Above: A commencement celebration, 1962. Pictured, from left, are Keuper, Florida Secretary of State Tom Adams, Astronaut Virgil "Gus" Grissom, and Florida State University Vice President Varner Baum. Adams, who would be given an honorary doctorate in space education, gave a fiery commencement address in support of the potential creation of Florida Christian University.

Left: From left, Harold Dibble holds BEC's first degree while Reagan Dubose is congratulated by Jerry Keuper for earning it. Dubose earned an associate's degree in engineering in 1961 and went on to earn a bachelor's degree from BEC.

Astronaut Virgil "Gus" Grissom receives the university's first honorary doctorate from Keuper, while Tom Putnam, the college's first full-time employee, adjusts his hood. Grissom's acceptance of an honorary doctorate in 1962 gave the young college great credibility among the scientists and engineers working at Cape Canaveral.

As history would note, the *Brevard Sentinel* jumped the gun in this celebration of the creation of Florida Christian University. There were many reasons why the merger with the Disciples of Christ Church didn't succeed, not the least of which was the church's insistence on new leadership for the college.

Brownlie Hall, Brevard Engineering College's first dormitory, shown here under construction, was completed in 1964. It marked the beginning of BEC as a residential college.

Brevard Engineering College's library was dedicated in January 1965 in honor of William Bartholomae. The two-story building was part of a boom of new construction instituted by the college during its first decade.

BEC's first chairman of the board, George Shaw.

Legendary rocket scientist Wernher von Braun reads a copy of the campus humor magazine during a visit to campus in June 1964.

Dr. J. Robert Oppenheimer, director of the Institute of Advanced Studies at Princeton University, lectured at BEC in 1965.

Frank Carey, left, chief test conductor on Project Gemini, shows his awards to Ray Work, one of Florida Tech's pioneering faculty members. Carey was one of the first graduates of Florida Tech, earning an electrical engineering degree.

The *Brevard Sentinel* announced Brevard Engineering College's name change to Florida Institute of Technology, 1966.

George Campbell, left, shakes hands with Jerry Keuper after Florida Institute of Technology completed the purchase of Campbell Aviation on September 22, 1968. The purchase led to the creation of FIT Aviation and the School of Aeronautics. Jerry Laudenaugh, right, helped to facilitate the deal.

FIT's athletics program took flight during the university's first decade. Here, FIT takes on MIT.

Board of Trustees Chairman Denton Clark, left, looks on as Keuper points out new construction, and plots new directions for the university's second decade.

Second Stage: A Decade of Growth, Expansion, and Gardening

Florida Institute of Technology, 1968–1978

By 1968, both Florida Institute of Technology and America's space program were on the cusp of the kind of success Jerome Keuper could have only dreamt of when he crossed the state line more than a decade earlier.

The great success of the space program was easy to see by 1969 when America won the race to the moon. The university's success was no less impressive, though quieter in nature.

The coming ten years would mark the first of two tremendous periods of growth for the university. This growth was realized in two ways: First, through new construction; and second, by the expansion of academic programs.

Many of the changes taking place on campus were hard to miss. In 1970, the university's first $1 million building was completed, the Crawford Science Tower. Fully seven stories high, it was and is the tallest building on campus, dominating the landscape on University Boulevard. Just two years later, the second of Florida Tech's two towers was completed, a dormitory christened Roberts Hall. Built at the very northern edge of campus, Roberts looms over the university's Country Club Drive entrance.

Keuper's fondness for growth was not limited to new construction. During the university's second decade, he undertook a historic expansion of the university's palm tree collection and created a nationally renowned botanical garden. The garden flourishes on campus to this day.

The last of the brick-and-mortar enhancements during this time came with the completion of the original residence quadrangle. The final piece of the puzzle was Evans Hall. Dedicated in 1976, the hall housed eighty-four women, a modern cafeteria, the Rathskellar Pub, and other student conveniences.

Other changes were more subtle. In 1974, a year made famous by a campus-wide streak, the university created its M.B.A. and Ph.D. programs in biology. The Biology Department was only two years old at

The Botanical Garden, at left, shown here after a renovation in 2007, took shape during the university's second decade. Students, above right, leave the student center at Florida Tech's Jensen Beach campus.

the time. Dr. Gary Wells, who chaired the department for more than two decades, was a founding faculty member in the department.

Florida Tech continued to attract the world's best scientists to campus, including Edward Teller, the father of the hydrogen bomb. Teller lectured on campus in 1977, and received the President's Medal.

That same year, the university opened a counseling center for students. The following year, a student health center opened in the Denius Student Center. Another expansion of student services in 1975 was the creation of the university's public radio station, WFIT.

When not constructing new buildings high into the sky, Keuper and a very active board of trustees were busy expanding the university's footprint beyond the campus's boundaries.

First, in 1972, the U.S. Navy paid the university the high honor of asking it to create an off-campus program in Maryland. Keuper happily complied, and University College was born. Later that same year, the university's four-year-old Hydrospace Technical Institute acquired an eighty-four-acre campus in Jensen Beach, Fla. The campus would educate technicians and technologists in marine and environmental fields for more than two decades. It would serve as the home of the new School of Marine and Environmental Technology.

Intercollegiate athletics continued to grow during Florida Tech's second decade, culminating with the university's inclusion into the National Collegiate Athletic Association in 1978. By the time Florida Tech joined the NCAA, the university had established a reputation in a number of sports, especially rowing. Under the direction of longtime Athletics Director Bill Jurgens, the team won the 1978 Southeast United States Crew Championship and competed in the prestigious Henley Royal Regatta. The crew program remains a national power to present day.

By the time the crew team crossed the ocean for this competition, the university it represented had truly set sail as well. Just twenty years old, Florida Institute of Technology was already the second-largest private university in Florida, and was recognized as the only private technological university in the Southeast.

Jensen Beach campus, above left, was acquired in 1972. The university's second decade was underway as men began to explore the moon, right.

SECOND STAGE: A DECADE OF GROWTH, EXPANSION, AND GARDENING | 29

An aerial view of the campus during the construction of the Crawford Science Tower, left. The tower, Florida Tech's first million-dollar building, was made possible in part by a donation from RCA, represented above by Denton Clark. The building was named for Dr. Frederick Crawford (top right, with Keuper).

Keuper (above), seen here in 1981, brought the Botanical Garden to Florida Tech during the university's second decade. His love of palm trees is legendary, and over the years, the Florida Tech campus was the beneficiary of this passion. Sharing this passion with Keuper was Dent Smith, left, for whom the Dent Smith Trail is named. Smith, a retired Wall Street executive, was a key contributor to Florida Tech's collection of rare palm trees, one of the largest such collections in the world.

Right: With the purchase of the Jensen Beach campus, the university was able to do more than get its feet wet in marine studies. At right, Jensen Beach students prepare for another research mission aboard the *Aquarius*. On the following page, more Jensen Beach students embark on a field trip in the Indian River Lagoon.

A group photo of the first biology faculty, circa 1972. Dr. Richard Turner, far left, is the only remaining original member on the faculty today. Dr. Gary Wells, fourth from right, was the department's head for more than two decades.

Edward Teller, father of the hydrogen bomb, speaks at Florida Tech's twentieth anniversary celebration. The celebration, named "Under the Palms," featured Teller as the keynote speaker. His bold message to the audience that evening was that FIT was poised to take the baton from MIT.

Campus life at Jensen Beach may have been more laid back than at the Melbourne campus, but the curriculum was equally as rigorous, and the campus produced very proud alumni.

It didn't take the newly minted Evans Dining Hall a long time to fill up with hungry students, faculty, and staff upon its opening in 1976. Ray Work, above, joins a group of students in enjoying the best Evans had to offer.

Denton Clark was a founding trustee of Florida Tech and served as the board's second chairman in the late 1960s and early 1970s. Clark spent twenty-five years on the Florida Tech board and is now a trustee emeritus.

During the university's second decade, Florida Tech continued to develop critical student life programs. In the photo above, President Keuper recognizes the contributions of Wayne Rardon '69, who served his senior year as the president of the Student Government Association.

SECOND STAGE: A DECADE OF GROWTH, EXPANSION, AND GARDENING | 39

Bill Jurgens, with bullhorn at far left, came to Florida Tech to coach the fledgling rowing teams and stayed for more than three decades, building a remarkable legacy as its athletics director in the process.

Keuper's campus building in the 1970s would take the Florida Tech brand to many places, including, as the banner at right shows, Lugano, Switzerland. Longtime admissions employee Bob Rowe sits underneath.

Florida Tech's student body began to change during its second decade. Most notable was the growth in percentage of female students on campus. Women, which could be counted on one hand (if not one finger) in the BEC's first classes, today represent nearly 40 percent of the student population.

Florida Tech's community outreach received a boost with the creation of WFIT, a student-run public radio station. The station has changed formats over the years but has remained an integral part of Brevard's radio landscape, providing, among other services, NPR news and programming. The station celebrated its thirtieth anniversary in 2005.

Traditions and Transition

Florida Institute of Technology, 1978–1988

Florida Institute of Technology's third decade was marked by continued growth in many areas of university life, but it was most notable as a time of seismic transition.

In 1985, Keuper retired after nearly thirty years at the helm of the university. During his last years in office, he led with the same energy and vigor he had demonstrated when founding the school a generation earlier. During Florida Tech's third decade, Keuper oversaw remarkable academic expansion at the university.

During Florida Tech's first twenty years, the administration focused largely on creating an infrastructure for the burgeoning institution. Then the focus shifted to creating the academic and athletic foundations necessary for long-term stability and growth.

Toward that end, Florida Tech added two new schools, which expanded the university's offerings from its core in engineering, aviation, and the sciences. With the creation of the School of Psychology and the School of Management and Humanities, Florida Tech had truly expanded its mission from that of an institute to one of a university. Reflective of this change in status was a change in the athletics mascot, as the Florida Tech Engineers were re-christened the Panthers.

However, this academic expansion did not mean that Florida Tech had turned its back on its foundation in engineering and the sciences.

Quite the opposite.

More than two dozen new degree programs and research institutes in

Left: A March 1982 launch of an INTELSAT V communications satellite on an Atlas Centaur Rocket. A well-lit Link Building is in the foreground. The Evans Library, above right, under construction.

engineering and the sciences were developed during the university's third decade. Notable among these were a forward-thinking master's program in computer education and a bachelor's program in aviation management, both started in 1983. By Florida Tech's fifth decade, the university's Computer Science Department would be world-renown, and aviation management would be the single most popular undergraduate major.

Florida Tech's changing student population was reflective of the change in the academic life of the university. Long gone were the days of dress codes and hair-length requirements instituted during the earlier years of the university. Some students, of course, maintained a short hair-length requirement, as the Army Reserved Officer Training Corps program blossomed during this time.

Outside of academic accomplishment, there were several milestones of note in Florida Tech's third decade. In 1981, the Republic of China presented the university with a sixteen-foot clock tower made of Taiwanese marble. This gift, given in memory of Chao Tsu-yu, former chairman of Taiwan's Vocational Assistance Commission for Retired Servicemen, also served as a celebration of Florida Tech's long history with the Taiwanese people.

Also in 1981, Florida Tech became affiliated with Hawthorne College, a liberal arts college in New Hampshire. The collaboration was ultimately short-lived, but nonetheless it remains an interesting footnote in the university's history.

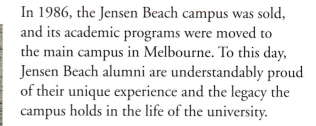

In 1983, the university celebrated its twenty-fifth anniversary. The event brought accolades from all over the nation to Florida Tech.

In 1986, the Jensen Beach campus was sold, and its academic programs were moved to the main campus in Melbourne. To this day, Jensen Beach alumni are understandably proud of their unique experience and the legacy the campus holds in the life of the university.

In athletics, Florida Tech joined the Sunshine State Conference, dedicated the Percy L. Hedgecock Gymnasium, and celebrated a rowing victory at the prestigious Dad Vail Regatta in Philadelphia.

Florida Tech's third decade ended with the university—having had one president in its first twenty-seven years—under the guidance of three presidents in its next three years. After Keuper retired in 1985, long-time vice president and physicist John Miller served the university he loved as president while the search committee conducted its important work.

In 1987, as Florida Tech's third decade came to a close, the committee announced its decision: Dr. Lynn Edward Weaver would be the third president of Florida Institute of Technology.

Above left: The unveiling of the clock tower. **At right:** Keuper speaks to a class in the early 1980s.

TRADITIONS AND TRANSITION | 45

Several Florida Tech students found the 1979 Homecoming raft race to be a complete washout.

Students in this 1979 photo study in Florida Tech's original library. The new Evans Library would be built six years later.

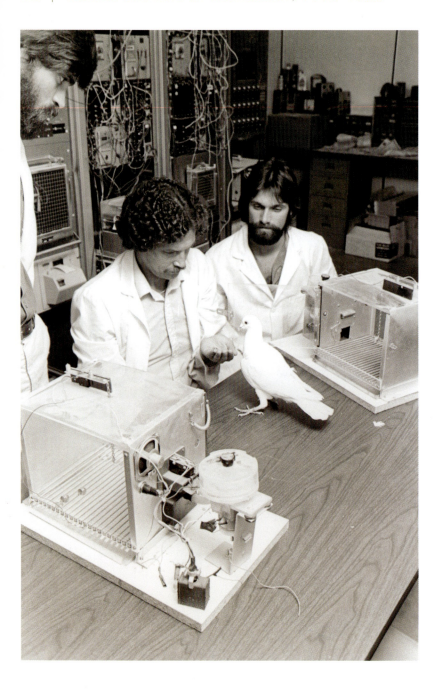

The new School of Psychology, along with its counterpart the School of Management and Humanities, propelled FIT to university status. In the picture on the left, Professor Art Gutman (center) works with Psy. D. graduate students Eric Zilmer, left, and Scott Heller. In the photo above, Founding Dean Charles Corman prepares the conference room with his assistant, Jani McCray. McCray still serves as the dean's assistant in the College of Psychology and Liberal Arts.

John Reynolds has been the women's basketball coach for more than two decades. Entering the 2007–08 season, Reynolds was closing in on 400 career victories, with a lifetime record of 377–201. Reynolds has been named Sunshine State Conference Coach of the Year on five separate occasions.

During the university's third decade, Florida Tech changed its athletics nickname from "Engineers" to "Panthers." The new nickname was decided by a vote of the student body.

Keuper's vision for Florida Tech extended well beyond the state of Florida. In the photo above, he meets with site directors for what was then known as Off Campus Programs. In this April 1982 photo are, top row from left, Ernest French, Harry Woods, Wayne Sills, Vincent Siragusa, Tom Loper, Bill Creed, Hugh Harrison, Len Winter, Bob Fleming, Conrad Davis, Tom Adkinson, and Ed Gugel. Bottom row, from left, Harry Weber, Keuper, Pat Sims, and Jim Stoms. Florida Tech was also among the first universities to begin distance education classes, using the videotape long before the invention of the Internet. In the photo at left, Phillip Horton's class is videotaped.

TRADITIONS AND TRANSITION | 51

Florida Tech's Computer Science Department traces its beginnings to the early 1980s. The university was rightly proud of its abilities in the newly growing field. These photos showcase the state-of-the-art technology of the day. Today, Florida Tech is a nationally recognized leader in computer science and is particularly strong in the areas of information assurance and software testing.

Florida Tech's ROTC program became a central part of student life during the university's third decade. Today, Florida Tech leads the nation in ROTC participation rate.

During the early 1980s, Florida Tech had a brief alliance with Hawthorne College in New England. The unlikely partnership between the technological university and the liberal arts college was short-lived, however.

Above: Keuper, left, congratulates long-time facilities management director Dale Simcox at the dedication of Simcox Square in January 1983.

Right: Department of Marine and Environmental Systems icons John Trefry, left, and Iver Duedall confer in September 1983. Duedall, with long-time colleague John Williams, would write a series of popular books on hurricanes and tropical storms, while Trefry would earn the 2002 Gold Medal from the Florida Academy of Sciences.

New buildings continued to go up during the university's third decade. Seen here in April 1981 is the groundbreaking of the O.A. Holzer Student Health Center. From left, Holzer's granddaughters Holly and Beth Holzer, Dr. Thomas Holzer, Dr. Oswald A. Holzer, Mary Holzer, and Ruth Alice Holzer. Oswald was the long-time director of Florida Tech's Student Health Center.

Keuper had plenty of help celebrating Florida Tech's twenty-fifth anniversary. In the photo above, Florida Governor Bob Graham and Barbara Newell, chancellor of the state university system, help Keuper cut the ceremonial cake.

In 1982, Florida Tech rowing celebrated a National Championship at the Dad Vail Regatta in Philadelphia. Here, team members showcase their awards and trophies back home in Melbourne.

Left: Unprecedented growth in the early 1980s would have unintended consequences, including long lines for class registration.

John Miller, above right, served the university with distinction as both a long-time vice president and as president, easing the transition from Keuper to Lynn Edward Weaver (christening a boat named in his honor, top left). Andy Revay, bottom left, seen here receiving an award from IEEE, served the university for more than three decades. Revay ended his career as the vice president for Academic Affairs for President Weaver.

Members of the Theta Xi fraternity celebrate winning first place for their float at the inaugural Florida Tech Homecoming Parade on February 18, 1984.

Jimmy Buffett played to a packed campus crowd on February 16, 1985. Evans Dining Hall featured Cheeseburgers in Paradise for dinner that evening.

Reaching for the Stars

Florida Institute of Technology, 1988–1998

When Lynn Edward Weaver took the reins as the third president of Florida Institute of Technology, he had three priorities. He wanted to improve the campus, expand the scope of Florida Tech's research mission, and most importantly, place the institution on solid financial footing.

To fund much-needed campus improvements, Florida Tech undertook a $25 million capital campaign during the first five years of the Weaver administration. Buoyed by a lead gift of $5 million from the Harris Corporation, the university's long-time ally, the successful campaign concluded in June of 1993.

The surge in funding led to many capital improvements on campus, including the George M. Skurla Building for the College of Aeronautics, a remodeled and expanded Panther Plaza, paved parking lots, and more lighting and sidewalks throughout the campus. An equally important improvement was the expansion, by thirty acres, of the southern end of campus. This purchase provided the land for the university's current baseball, softball, and soccer fields.

Weaver's concentration on scientific inquiry led to the creation of a vice president for research position and the purchase and construction of new buildings designed for this purpose. The change was a dramatic cultural shift for an institution that had, since its inception, emphasized teaching. But Weaver was steadfast in his determination to evolve Florida Tech into a research university, and today, Florida Tech's research capabilities are world renowned.

Ironically, it was a rejected funding request during the campaign that changed the university forever. In 1990, Weaver unsuccessfully

President Lynn Edward Weaver, above right, surveys the construction of the F.W. Olin Engineering Building.

approached the F.W. Olin Foundation for a $5 million gift for a new engineering building. Despite the rejection, this request began a strong, long-term relationship between Florida Tech's leadership and the foundation's president, Lawrence W. Milas. When the foundation decided to fundamentally change its strategy and throw its considerable financial weight behind a single institution, Florida Tech was a prime candidate.

As Weaver recounted the story, in 1995 Milas came to him and asked a question most college presidents only dream of hearing: "What would Florida Tech do with a lot of money?"

Two years later, Florida Tech, and the world, found out the answer.

In 1997, the F.W. Olin Foundation announced the single largest gift in its history: $50 million to Florida Tech. The money was divided three ways. First, $21 million was set aside for the construction of the F.W. Olin Engineering Complex and the F.W. Olin Life Sciences Building. Second, $4 million was given to the College of Engineering for faculty chairs, fellowships, and scholarships. Finally, $25 million was pledged as a challenge grant, a matching donation to the university's endowment, dollar for dollar.

Taken alone, the gift of the buildings would have been the largest in the university's history. Its significance cannot be overstated, as it immediately provided the campus with 100,000 square feet of classroom, laboratory, and office space, as well as created a fulcrum for a newly emergent south campus.

Ten years into his tenure, Weaver skillfully grabbed the golden ring, and Florida Tech was changed forever.

In the photo above, the groundbreaking of the F.W. Olin Engineering Building. At right, Biological Sciences Professor Junda Lin works with students in his marine biology lab.

Florida Tech's College Players have long provided comedy and drama to the faculty, students, and staff of the university. In the photos above and left, members of the College Players prepare during a March 1997 dress rehearsal for "Much Ado About Nothing."

Above: The construction of the F.W. Olin buildings necessitated the move of the Panthers' baseball, softball, and soccer fields. The photo above shows the new baseball field, named for Panther legends Les Hall and Andy Seminick.

Right: Florida Tech's soccer program gained elite status during the university's fourth decade. Under Head Coach Rick Stottler, the men's soccer team won Division II national titles in 1988 and, in the photo at right, 1991.

Following Page: Florida Tech's engineering students and faculty earned national recognition during the university's fourth decade. In 1991, a student team competed in the General Motors–sponsored Sunrayce with the Solar 1.

Weaver made state and nationally funded research a priority during his tenure as president. This focus led to remarkable discoveries, including one made by the team featured at right. Biology Professor Glenn Cohen, left, and Harris Professor of Engineering Fred Ham worked together to create a painless way for diabetes patients to measure insulin levels. Weaver also brought to campus Joshua Rokach to head the university's Claude Pepper Institute. Rokach's research focuses on preventing arterial disease.

One of Weaver's first decisions was to immediately embark on a $25 million, five-year capital campaign. The campaign, which concluded in 1992, was a success, thanks in large part to a $5 million gift by the Harris Corporation. Harris Corporation evolved from Radiation, Inc., one of the many Space Coast companies that embraced the university upon its inception in 1958. Showing off the check, above, are Capital Campaign Chairman Jack Pruitt, Harris Corporation CEO Jack Hartley, and Florida Tech President Lynn Edward Weaver. Hartley, above right, made the formal announcement of the gift in April of 1988.

Above: A $1.2 million grant from the Federal Aviation Administration made possible the construction of the George M. Skurla Building, the home of the College of Aeronautics. Dedicated in 1991, the building was named for the university's board of trustees member and retired president and CEO of Grumman Corporation. In the 1960s, Skurla led the team that put the finishing touches on the Eagles that landed on the moon.

Right: Florida Tech and the F.W. Olin Foundation announce a historic gift to the university. From left, F.W. Olin Foundation Chairman Lawrence Milas, Weaver, and Florida Tech Chairman of the Board Jack Hartley.

The Edge of Discovery

Florida Institute of Technology, 1998–2007

Florida Institute of Technology's fifth decade opened with a promising beginning and closed with the fulfillment of that promise.

On January 15, 1998, the first ceremonial scoops of earth were turned on the new F.W. Olin Engineering Complex and the F.W. Olin Life Sciences Building. With this simple exercise, Florida Tech was transformed at the dawn of the twenty-first century.

The groundbreaking, and the buildings it gave rise to, did more than add 100,000 square feet to the campus footprint. It brought the full prestige of the F.W. Olin Foundation upon Florida Tech, and this imprimatur would help the university enjoy a decade of unprecedented fund-raising success.

The university's fifth decade was bookended by two successful capital campaigns, led by two presidents of remarkable vision.

First, buoyed by the F.W. Olin challenge grant, Dr. Lynn Edward Weaver led the university on the Campaign for a Rising Star. The campaign provided Florida Tech with long-sought-after financial stability and two impressive new buildings on south campus. The endowment match campaign led to phenomenal growth in the university's endowment, from $1 million in 1997 to more than $32 million by the close of the campaign in 2002.

The university's south campus was equally transformed by the campaign. In addition to buildings for engineering and life sciences, the campaign led to the construction of the Charles and Ruth Clemente Center for Sports and Recreation and the creation of the F.W. Olin Athletics Complex, home of the Florida Tech baseball, softball, and soccer programs.

The end of the campaign provided the university with an unexpected bonus, a $14 million building dedicated to chemistry, physics, and space sciences. The completion of the

For fifty years, Florida Tech has had strong roots in America's space program. NASA astronaut and Florida Tech alumna Sunita Williams (above, at right) spent the first six months of 2006 aboard the International Space Station. Joining her on the voyage to the station was fellow alumna Joan Higginbotham (above, at left). Florida Tech alumnus George Zamka piloted the shuttle in October 2007.

F.W. Olin Physical Sciences Building placed the grand total of financial support from the foundation at a staggering $60 million.

The conclusion of the Campaign for a Rising Star also marked a successful end to Weaver's fifteen-year tenure at the university. For the second time, the university's future was placed in the hands of a presidential search committee, and once again, Florida Tech struck gold.

On July 1, 2002, Dr. Anthony James Catanese became the fourth president of Florida Institute of Technology. Upon his arrival, Catanese immediately announced an ambitious agenda for Florida Tech, one designed to achieve his goal of the university becoming one of the ten best institutes of technology in the world.

Under Catanese's direction, the university's research funding tripled, and Florida Tech began the most ambitious fund-raising campaign in its history, the Golden Anniversary Campaign. The campaign's $50 million goal was announced at a black tie gala in April of 2007.

Surpassing its goal, the campaign funded a new center at the Melbourne International Airport for FIT Aviation, a new building for the College of Psychology and Liberal Arts, and the Harris Center for Science and Engineering.

Student housing, much of which had been built decades earlier, was completely overhauled during the Catanese presidency. First, the university dedicated Columbia Village in 2003. Each of the seven buildings was dedicated to the memory of one of the Space Shuttle Columbia's seven astronauts.

In 2007, construction began on new housing on the campus's south end. Completed in 2008, this new complex is home to 385 students. Its completion is just part of a remarkable bricks-and-mortar renaissance on campus. As Florida Tech's fifth decade came to a close, more than half of the buildings on campus had been built in those last ten years.

By 2008, a university born of the space age had truly come of age. Growing in student population, research funding, endowment, and prestige, Florida Tech closed out its fifth decade as a transformed institution, one uniquely positioned to serve Florida, America, and the world.

Two hurricanes—Frances and Jeanne—were unwelcome guests in the fall of 2004.

The dedication of Florida Tech's new baseball field in honor of Les Hall and Andy Seminick brought out many well wishers, including, from left, Les Hall (at podium), Florida Tech alumnus and Boston Red Sox star Tim Wakefield, athletics pioneer and Philadelphia Phillie Andy Seminick, F.W. Olin Foundation Chairman Lawrence Milas, Florida Tech Chairman of the Board Jack Hartley, and President Lynn Edward Weaver.

Florida Tech's Campaign for a Rising Star, initiated by an F.W. Olin Foundation gift, was capped with another gift from the foundation, this time for $14 million. This final gift led to the construction of the F.W. Olin Physical Sciences Building, home of the dean of the College of Science and the Departments of Chemistry and Physics and Space Sciences. The research telescope atop the building is the largest in the state of Florida.

Another important part of that campaign was the construction of the Charles and Ruth Clemente Center for Sports and Recreation, at right. Clemente, a Florida Tech board member, is fifth from left and standing next to his wife, Ruth, in the above groundbreaking photo.

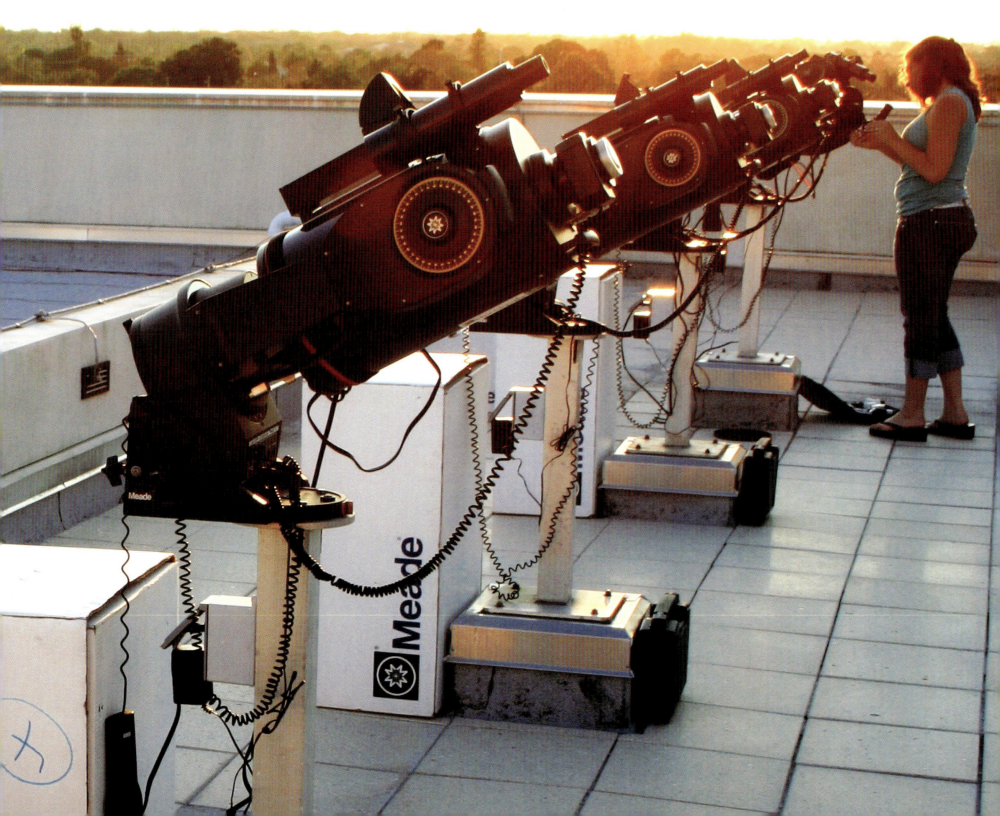

Florida Tech's fourth president, Anthony J. Catanese, made a priority of restoring Florida Tech's Botanical Garden to its previous glory.

Preceding page: Telescopes line the roof of the F.W. Olin Physical Sciences Building as a student prepares for an astronomy lab.

Weaver's retirement led to the hiring of Catanese in the summer of 2002. In the above photo, the two men pose in front of the Clemente Center after the press conference introducing Catanese. Catanese, an avid marathoner, ran with the cross country team that same fall to proclaim his presidency, "off and running."

Under Catanese, the university began to establish its identity as a place where undergraduate students could learn and do nationally funded research with faculty members. The concept of "High Tech with a Human Touch" became a cornerstone of the Catanese administration, and events like the student design showcase (above and right) became annual celebrations of student achievement. Adam Linsenbardt '06 shows off the Aurora at right.

One student design project made history in June 2006, as the Panther 1 was the first student-built rocket to launch from Cape Canaveral. Named for the Florida Tech mascot, Panther 1 was a complete success. After launch, it followed a perfect parabolic path to a splashdown in the Atlantic.

THE EDGE OF DISCOVERY | 87

Both fund-raising and athletics have been a priority for Catanese. In his first year as president, he announced the addition of five new sports at Florida Tech. These included men's and women's golf, men's and women's tennis, and women's soccer. Growing with Florida Tech's athletic programs is its fund-raising prowess. The Sporting Affair fund-raiser for athletics scholarships, highlighted by the Chopper Dropper (below and right), raises upwards of $250,000 each year.

The Golden Anniversary Campaign for Florida Tech, with a goal of $50 million, is the largest in the university's history. In the photo above, President Catanese, with wife Sara, center, and donor Ruth Funk, celebrate at the public kickoff of the campaign. The Golden Anniversary kickoff brought together a generation of leadership for Florida in the photo at right. From left, Phillip W. Farmer, Chairman of the Board of Trustees and the Golden Anniversary Campaign; Jeanne Farmer, President Catanese; Sara Catanese; Martha Hartley, and former Chairman of the Board Jack Hartley.

In October of 2003, Florida Institute of Technology dedicated a new residence hall complex to the memory of the Space Shuttle Columbia and her seven-person crew. This dedication was the result of an idea put forward by the Student Government Association and strongly endorsed by Catanese (speaking at the dedication, above).

An overflow crowd, filled with faculty, staff, students, media, and members of each of the seven families personally affected by the Columbia tragedy were on hand at the dedication. William Readdy (facing page at right), NASA associate administrator for Space Flight, tied the connection between America's space program and the university founded by rocket scientists. He said, "Florida Tech prepares students to explore, not only academically, but to explore life, and prepares them to be future leaders and the explorers of the generation to come. I can think of no more fitting tribute for [Columbia Astronauts] Rick, William, David, Michael, Laurel, Kalpana, and Ilan than dedicating these residence halls at the Florida Institute of Technology."

In 2007, sophomore women's golfer Daniela Iacobelli earned Florida Tech's first individual national championship, winning the tournament with a five-over 293. Iacobelli's NCAA Division II championship came in just the fourth year of the Panthers' women's golf program.

They were there at the beginning and have been eyewitnesses to the growth of a fifty-year-old marvel. George Shaw, left, and Denton Clark pose in front of the F.W. Olin Physical Sciences Building, in celebration of their instrumental roles in the life of the university.

Passing the Torch

Florida Institute of Technology, 2008

During its first fifty years, Florida Institute of Technology has grown from being a great story to becoming an excellent institution. Along the way, it has attracted world-renowned engineers, scientists, and scholars to its doors. Florida Tech counts among its alumni some of the best and brightest minds the world has to offer.

Now we are focused on the next fifty years—and beyond—for Florida Tech. By the end of our fifty-first year, the university will have completed another major transformation of the campus with the construction of the South Village. The changes in its physical environment are readily apparent. It is safe to say that no American university has grown and prospered as much as Florida Tech during the past decade.

With a remarkable physical infrastructure in place, the university is now beginning a transformation that will not be so easy to see.

During the next fifty years, Florida Tech will emerge as a leading research institution in engineering and science research across a broad spectrum of fields. Look for Florida Tech to prosper in the computer sciences, bio-engineering, aviation, the marine sciences, engineering, and yes, the future of rocket science.

Its student body will grow, but the growth on the main campus will be measured, with no more than 5,000 students. As a university firmly rooted in technology, Florida Tech will reach twenty-first-century students in their homes or at their offices through distance education. The Internet is the next great classroom, and Florida Tech students will shine there as well.

Our students will continue to excel on the playing fields. We often joke of our undefeated football program, but our success in fifteen men's and women's sports is no joke. Athletic success will continue, and new sports will be added, including swimming and diving. Who knows, one day Florida Tech may be home to an NCAA surfing champion.

Finally, Florida Tech's roots are firmly in America's space program. The university will be a part of the space program well into the future, doing research and providing the next generation of astronauts, rocket scientists, and engineers to help America take the next leap forward into the final frontier—to Mars and beyond!

Anthony James Catanese, Ph.D. FAICP
President
May 1, 2008

Three buildings in total, the new residence halls loom over the university's soccer fields. The newest residence halls at Florida Tech provided the centerpiece for the university's new South Village. The South Village served as the realization of a vision of Florida Tech President Anthony J. Catanese. Catanese developed the area to reflect the new urbanism movement.

Florida Tech's South Village, the vision of President Anthony J. Catanese, will feature a new aquatics center, dining facility, parking garage, the Scott Center for Autism Treatment, the Harris Center for Science and Engineering, and three new residence halls.

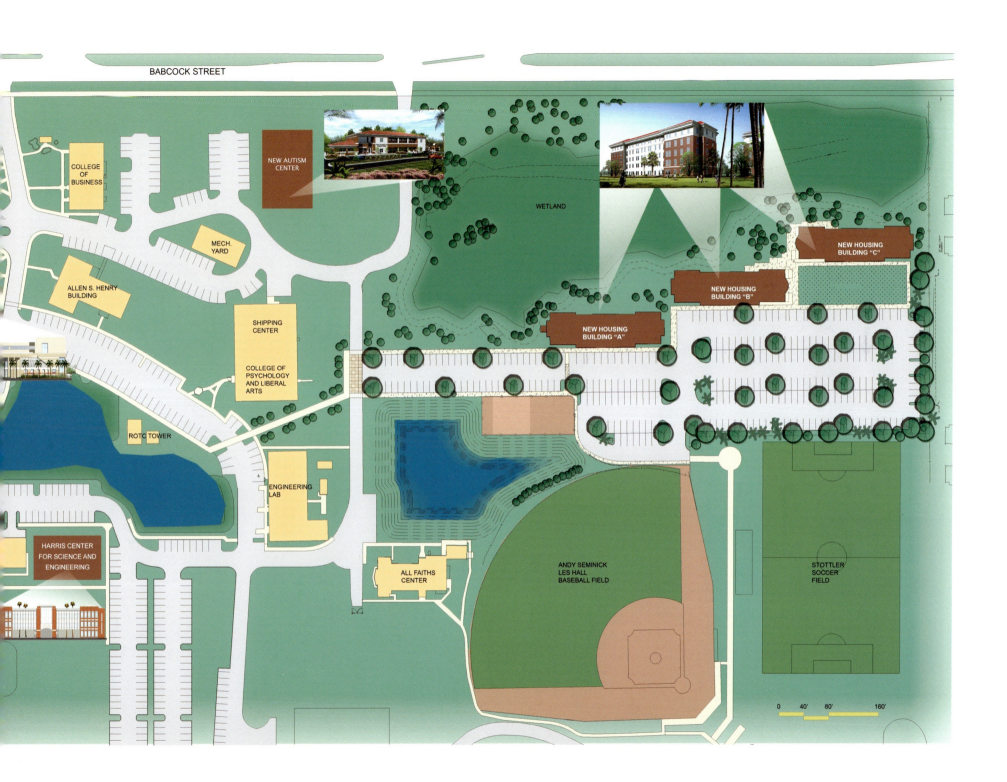

The new Florida Tech aquatics center will be located next to the Charles and Ruth Clemente Center for Sports and Recreation. The center will feature an Olympic-sized swimming pool and integrated diving well.

A new dining hall will be an important part of the South Village. Located next to the aquatics center, this facility will provide easy access for the nearly 400 residents of the new residence halls on south campus.

The Emil Buehler Center for Aviation Training and Research is under construction at Melbourne International Airport. The new center will provide classroom and laboratory space for the College of Aeronautics as well as a new Fixed Base Operation for FIT Aviation. It will also serve as the home of Florida Tech's new fleet of airplanes.

The Scott Center for Autism Treatment at Florida Tech will be constructed east of the School of Psychology Building on Babcock Street. The center will ultimately provide services for hundreds of autistic children and provide behavioral psychology students an invaluable arena for critical research on autism.

The Ruth Funk Center for Textile Arts, made possible by a generous gift by Florida Tech trustee Ruth Funk, will nestle alongside the Evans Library in the heart of the university's north campus.

A new parking garage located behind the dining hall will fulfill a continuous campus need for more parking.

Appendix B

Five Decades of Florida Institute of Technology Trustees

Mr. Tom Adams	1965–1974	Ms. Jane Carey Gleason	1995–2002	Mr. Allan M. Norton	1990–1992
Mr. Robert C. Allen	1975–1983	Mr. George Gourlay	1993–1999	Mr. Gerald T. Oppliger	1992–1997
Mr. Richard H. Anschutz	1978–1988	Mr. Douglas E. Graves	1964	Dr. Robert E. Payne	1966–1967
Mr. William E. Arnold	1978–1980	Lady Marie-Louise Grundy	1983–1988	Mr. W.J. Pettigrew	1962–1967
Mr. Norman G. Bitterman	1959–1960	Mr. Jack Hazard	1958	Mr. George W. Phelps	1973–1982
Rev. Alex Boyer	1959–1973	Mr. Howard N. Hebert	1987–1991	Mr. Randall E. Poliner	2000–2007
Mr. Jack W. Boykin	1987–1994	Mr. Percy Hedgecock	1981–1987	Mr. Richard D. Pope, Sr.	1976–1978
Mr. R.L. Brickford	1962	Mr. Wilbur C. Henderson	1996–2008	Mr. Garrett Quick	1958–1963
Mr. Hugh M. Brown	1993–1998	Mr. George W. Hepworth	1968–1985	Mr. Fred S. Roberts	1964–1975
Mr. Thomas R. Brown, Jr.	1964–1967	Dr. George K. Hess, Jr.	1963–1968	Ms. Caroline Rossetter	1983–1999
Mr. C. Robert Brown	1959–1960	Maj. Gen. David M. Jones	1973–1978	Dr. Albert R. Schroter	1984–1985
Mr. George S. Cherniak	1963–1965	Mr. James G. Kennedy, Jr.	1994–2002	Mr. Donald L. Shepherd	1979–1980
Mr. David L. Clayton	2001–2008	Dr. Jerome P. Keuper	1958–2002	Ms. Helen I. Shepherd	1980–1990
Mr. Wendell C. Colson	1990–1994	Mr. Vincent S. Lamb, Jr.	1983–1991	Mr. George M. Skurla	1979–2001
Mr. Edward J. DeBartolo	1985–1988	Mr. Douglas C. Lane	2002–2007	Mr. H. Earl Smalley	1983–1985
Dr. Homer R. Denius	1967–2006	Mr. David C. Latham	1970–1987	Ms. Judith Sample Smith	1995–2001
Mr. William C. Demetree	1985–2002	Mr. P. Scott Linder	1985–1987	Mr. Vincent E. Spezzano	1991–1999
Dr. Harold Dibble	1958–1962	Dr. Edwin A. Link	1973–1981	Mr. J.B. Stancliffe	1975–1977
Mr. Edward D. Duda	1989–1996	Mr. Robert L. Long	1999–2006	Dr. John Sterner	1958
Mr. Herman C. Eberts	1972–1978	Mr. James E. Lyons	1972–1987	Mr. Fred E. Sutton	1987–1990
Mrs. Florence Evans	1973–1978	Mr. Norman S. Lund, Sr.	1958–1972	Mr. Robert Thomas	1985–1987
Dr. Ralph S. Evinrude	1973–1986	Mr. B.G. MacNabb	1959–1963	Mr. O.E. Tibbs	1963–1967
Mr. George Faenza	1991–1997	Mr. Clifford E. Mattox	1958–1976	Mr. Vikram Verma	2001–2007
Mr. Charles R. Faust	1985–1987	Mr. James E. Matthews	1978–1980	Dr. Lynn E. Weaver	1987–2002
Mr. J.J. Finnegan	1959–1964	Dr. James R. Maxfield, Jr.	1977–1984	Mr. Charles F. West	1969–1981
Mr. William Fletcher	1965–1972	Lt. Gen. Forrest S. McCartney	1988–1998	Col. R.H. Workman	1959
Mr. Samuel J. Foosaner	1981	Mr. Kenneth M. McLaren	1959–1973	Dr. Samuel S. Wright	1959–1962
Ms. Karen M. Garrison	2001–2006	Mr. Roland Merrell	1974–1992	Mr. A. Thomas Young	1987–1989
Mr. Walter J. Gatti	1995–1997	Mr. Allen H. Neuharth	1995–1998		
Mrs. Victoria Gildred	1980–1987	Mr. Copeland D. Newbern	1981–1993		

Appendix A

The Florida Institute of Technology Board of Trustees, March 2008

Dr. Raymond A. Armstrong
Dr. Richard N. Baney
Dr. Joseph A. Boyd (Emeritus)
Mr. Harry Brandon
Mr. Albino Campanini
Mr. Joseph Caruso
Dr. Anthony J. Catanese
Dr. Andrew M. Clark
Mr. G. Denton Clark (Emeritus)
Mr. Charles Clemente
Mr. Martin E. Dandridge
Mr. Dale A. Dettmer
Mr. Phillip W. Farmer
Dr. James L. Fisher (Emeritus)
Mr. Joseph M. Flammio
Mrs. Ruth E. Funk
Mr. John T. Hartley
Mr. Henry Heflich
Dr. Allen S. Henry

Mr. Bjornar Hermansen
Mr. Erik E. Joh
Mr. Malcolm Kirschenbaum
Mr. Howard L. Lance
Ms. Marilyn C. Link (Emeritus)
Mr. Richard P. McNeight
Mr. William C. Potter
Mr. James E. Pruitt
Mr. Kenneth P. Revay
Mr. Michael Scafati
Mr. Edward W. Scott, Jr.
Mr. Scott J. Seymour
Mr. George S. Shaw (Emeritus)
Mr. John L. Slack
Mr. F. Alan Smith
Ms. Elizabeth "Jonnie" Swann
Mr. James W. Thomas